TEN DRAMA DISCUSSIONS
FOR YOUNG PEOPLE

RAY JACKSON

First published in 1996 by
KEVIN MAYHEW LTD
Rattlesden
Bury St Edmunds
Suffolk IP30 0SZ

0 1 2 3 4 5 6 7 8 9

ISBN 0 86209 924 2
Catalogue No 1500084

Cover by Fred Chevalier

Edited by David Gatward
Typesetting by Louise Hill
Printed in Great Britain by
Caligraving Limited Thetford Norfolk

Contents

To Chris, Sharon and Grant.

Just three names to you,
but the whole world to me.

Acknowledgements

My thanks go first to my family, for their never-ending love and support. My wife suffered the worst of my grumpiness – I hate being disturbed when I'm writing – and, as always, I am ever grateful for her love and patience. My daughter and son never seem to doubt that I will succeed at whatever I set out to do. This is tremendously supportive, I only wish I had some of their confidence!

I would like to express my thanks to David Gatward. Without his encouragement and his extremely positive response to my initial idea, this book would never have been started.

I am also grateful to Keith Topham, both for the crash course in poetry and for his invaluable help with the sketch, 'What Hope Is There For Man?' If you think my efforts at writing poetry are not terribly good, you should have seen my first attempt!

I believe that the members of Stage II (both past and present) deserve a special mention. I have expressed my thanks for their contribution to this book in my Introduction, but my gratitude goes much deeper than this. I have received from them far more than I could ever give.

Introduction

These sketches and debates were written to fill a need, a need for material which would enable a group of young people:

1. to have fun
2. to explore the issues which face society
3. to understand better the difficult decisions faced by those in authority
4. to be fully involved in the group through debate

Each chapter of this book takes the form of a simple sketch or presentation, followed by details of a related issue for group discussion. These group discussion pages have been designed to be photocopied, with the intention that copies can then be distributed amongst the group, and permission for photocopying for this purpose is hereby given. Similarly, permission for photocopying the scripts for the use of those participating in the sketches is also included.

The discussions in this book have been planned to amuse young people and to stimulate debates on a number of social and ethical problems. The nature of these problems means that there are no right or wrong answers and, at the end of the debate, the group leader may need to be ready to address any questions raised.

Perhaps this is an appropriate point to express my gratitude to Stage II (the Christian youth group of which I am a leader) for performing these sketches with such enthusiasm. Without their encouragement, this book would not have been written.

The Future, Pork Bellies and All That

Two or three chairs face the audience (or, preferably, a garden bench similar to a small park bench, if one is available). 'A' enters, sits down, crosses his legs, opens a newspaper, and begins to read. A moment later, 'B' enters and copies exactly what 'A' has done except that 'B' opens and reads a comic. *(Can also be used for concealing the scripts!)* Note that the newspaper and comic must be held high so that the audience can see what it is they are reading.

A   *(Lowering the newspaper and looking at the back of the comic.)* Are you still reading those silly comics?

B   *(Lowering comic.)* I don't read them really, I just look at the pictures.

A   You'd be better reading newspapers instead of those worthless comics. I keep telling you, a sound knowledge of current affairs can take you a long way in this world.

B   Oh yeah, well it hasn't taken you very far, has it? In fact, 20p for the bus would take you a darn sight further!

A   *(Replies slowly and disdainfully.)* I was speaking metaphorically.

B   Oh. Right. Well, don't take any notice of me then, 'cause I was speaking truthfully!

A   You ought to realise that some people have made a fortune by using their knowledge of current affairs. For instance, with the current beef crisis, I think we ought to be buying pork bellies.

B   Buying what?

A   Pork bellies, they're commodities, another name for futures.

B   Futures? *(Thinks for a moment.)* Naw, I've never heard of 'em. I've heard of presents though, I like presents!

A   *(Sarcastically.)* Ha, ha. For your information, futures are a means of speculating on the future value of commodities. So if you buy pork bellies today, all you need to do is wait until the price goes up and then you can sell them at a profit.

B   Listen, if I was buying pork bellies today, I'd want to eat them today, I am starving!

A   Sometimes you're just plain daft. I can't even hold a sensible conversation with you. *(Returns to reading the paper.)*

B   *(After a pause, not at all offended.)* Anyway, where would we keep 'em?

A   *(Puzzled, lowering his paper.)* Keep what?

B   These pork bellies you're on about, we've nowhere to keep 'em.

A   *(Shakes his head.)* No, you don't understand. You don't have to keep them anywhere. You're not actually buying them the way you would buy meat from a butcher, you don't have them delivered or anything like that.

B   You mean you don't actually get them? You're saying that you buy something that you don't get? What sort of a deal is that?

A   Don't think of it as a deal or a purchase, think of it as an investment.

B   It sounds more like a con trick to me! *(Laughs.)* Have you ever thought about buying rainbows? I'm doing a good deal on rainbows at the moment!

A   No, it's not like that at all. When you invest in futures, it's not like buying things to take home with you, you're just buying and selling to make a profit. If you get it right and the world price goes up, you can make millions.

B   And presumably, if it goes down, you're stuck with a boat load of pork bellies!

A   Look, it's not just pork bellies, it's a whole range of commodities. For example, you could buy copper.

B   Copper? I don't want copper! Why on earth would I want to buy copper?

A   *(Exasperated.)* Look, you don't buy commodities because you *want* them, you buy commodities so you can *sell* them again at a profit.

B   But I thought you said that you never get these things that you buy?

A   That's right, you don't.

B   Well, if you haven't got them, how on earth can you sell them?

A   Why do you always make things difficult? Can't you understand that what you're buying and selling is the *future* ownership of these commodities. That's why they're called futures!

B   *(After a thoughtful pause.)* Oh, I think I understand. Let me see if I've got this right. You *buy* these things that you *don't want*, but that's not a problem because you don't get them anyway, and then, at some time in the future, you *sell* all the things you *haven't got* and – hopefully – you make a fortune!

A   That's not quite how I would have put it, but it's right enough I suppose.

B   So dealing in futures amounts to buying things you don't want and selling things you haven't got!

A   *(Glumly.)* I suppose it does, yes.

B   So what's the *point* of it all?

A   Well, it all started so that farmers could get a guaranteed price for their harvest. The deals were arranged so that the farmers could sell their crops *before* they were harvested, then they didn't have to worry about price fluctuations at harvest time.

B So the farmers knew well in advance how much income they would have?

A Exactly!

B Well, I can understand a company which produces, say, pork pies, wanting to buy next year's supply of pork bellies from a farmer. That makes sense for the company, because it gives them a reliable supply of meat, and it helps the farmer, because he then knows he's sold all his produce. But why would anyone else want to buy and sell all these futures when they have no interest in the produce at all?

A It's just the way of the world, me old pal. Once there's a market for something – anything, in fact – there will always be people who want to trade in it, buying and selling it to make a profit. In other words, if you could convince enough people that the future value of rainbows will be higher than it is today, you could indeed sell people rainbows!

B So these traders don't actually produce anything then, they just buy and sell and make a big profit in the process?

A That's it.

B In fact, I bet they often make a bigger profit than the farmers and the pork pie makers?

A I shouldn't be at all surprised.

B It just seems wrong somehow, that the people who don't make or produce anything make the biggest profit, while those who supply people's needs have to struggle for survival. Where's the justice in the world, that's what I want to know? Where's the justice in the world?

GROUP DISCUSSION

Many aspects of the world seem unjust. While the wealthy nations generate vast profits through buying and selling the world's produce, the poorer nations cannot even buy sufficient to feed their populations. Throughout history the more wealthy nations have exploited the poorer, and for Christians especially this raises the whole difficult question of the use (or misuse) of wealth.

For this discussion, the group is being asked to play the part of the governors of the University of Dunlerning, a small independent college of excellence which was established on the previously quiet and sparsely populated (but now deserted) Scottish island of Werleeven.

Since the appointment of the new principal, a local man renowned for his strict control of spending, the university finds itself in the fortunate position of having surplus funds. Since this is likely to continue to be the case over the coming years, a meeting of the governors has been called to discuss the allocation of these funds and to agree an order of priority for the short-listed items of proposed expenditure described below.

University of Dunlerning

Proposed Items of Future Expenditure:

A

Increase the salaries of women lecturers to bring them into line with their male colleagues. (Currently, women earn approximately 12.5 per cent less than men for the same job.)

B

Construct and equip a new library for the university. (Currently, the so-called library is located in the hold of an old fishing trawler, moored in the small harbour which serves the university. Using the library is difficult in the winter when the sea is often choppy, even in the harbour, and especially unpleasant in the summer, when the smell of long-dead fish seems to cling to the books.)

C

Construct and equip a new sports complex for the use of both students and staff. (Currently, the only provision for exercise is the scenic, well-worn, cliff-top path to the now deserted village – and to the island's only pub.)

D

Provide crèche facilities for the children of both students and staff. (At present it is impossible for single parents to attend or to work at the university because of the lack of crèche facilities on the island.)

E

Establish a computer resource facility for the use of both students and lecturers. (Currently, the only computers available for the use of students are located in the computer studies department, which is situated in the library.)

F

Initiate a system of grants to encourage students from low-income families to attend the university. (Currently, only students from very wealthy families seem to find the university attractive. It has been suggested that this is because beer is £10 a pint in the island's only pub – the landlord of which seems to bear an uncanny resemblance to the university's new principal.)

G

Modify the buildings of the university to permit disabled students to attend. (This will involve widening doorways, providing ramps at changes in level, and installing a bosun's chair to the library and computer studies department.)

Jobs for the Boys

Two young men, old school friends, are talking in a pub about the people they know and the jobs these people have found. *(It is particularly important with this sketch that only the actors, and not the audience, have copies of the script.)*

Max   You found a job yet, Lofty?

Lofty   Naw, I've applied for the few jobs I've seen advertised but it's a waste of time, I never even get a reply. *(Shakes his head sadly.)* There ain't no jobs for the likes of you and me, Max.

Max   What about the other lads? Did any of them get fixed up? I bet Bob's doing all right, he got four good 'A' levels ya know!

Lofty   Funny you should mention him, I saw him only last week in the 'Rose and Crown' – first time for ages.

Max   What's he doing now then?

Lofty   He told me he's out nights as an egg grader.

Max   Phew! That's not much of a job for someone with four good 'A' levels! What sort of a job is grading eggs for someone like Bob?

Lofty   Grading eggs? He doesn't grade eggs, who said anything about grading eggs?

Max   You just did!

Lofty   I did not!

Max   Yes you did! You said he went out nights as an egg grader!

Lofty   I *didn't* say he went out nights as an egg grader, I said he went out nights as an egg *raider*! He goes out stealing eggs from poultry houses then he sells them at car boot sales!

Max   Blimey! That's terrible! Fancy Bob resorting to stealing; I can hardly believe it!

Lofty   Sign of the times that, Max, me old mate!

Max   I guess so. *(Sips beer and ponders for a moment.)* What about Jonesy, have you seen him lately?

Lofty   Oh, yeah, I see him all the time. He gets around a bit does old Jonesy! He's built up quite an empire now, ya know.

Max   Ay, that doesn't surprise me. I thought he would make a businessman, he always was a clever lad!

Lofty   Yeah, there's no flies on Jonesy!

Max   What's he doing then?

Lofty   Oh, they say he's big in imported rugs.

Max   Well, at least he's done all right for himself.

Lofty   Well, that's a matter of opinion! Personally, I think it's the pits!

Max   Why's that? What's wrong with importing rugs?

Lofty   Importing rugs? Who said anything about importing rugs?

Max   You did, you've just said it!

Lofty   I said nothing of the sort!

Max   Yes you did. You said, he's big in imported rugs! They were your exact words!

Lofty	That's not what I said at all!
Max	Yes you did!
Lofty	I didn't! What I said was, he's big in imported *drugs*!
Max	Oh! . . . You mean he's a drugs dealer?
Lofty	That's what the word is on the street!
Max	The rat! I can hardly believe it!
Lofty	Sad old world, isn't it?
Max	It certainly is.
Lofty	*(Sips beer, then after a pause.)* Do you remember Steve?
Max	You mean Steve the artist?
Lofty	Yeah, that's him. Well, I saw him in the 'Red Lion' the other day.
Max	He was brilliant, wasn't he? Do you remember those cartoons he drew of all the teachers? He was so gifted.
Lofty	Yeah, he could paint or draw anything and it just looked so real!
Max	Didn't he go to art college?
Lofty	Yeah, he did a four-year course, finished it last year. He's a qualified commercial artist now.
Max	Yeah, and I bet he's a good one too. I suppose he works for some graphic design studio now, does he?
Lofty	Naw, he went into printing.
Max	Oh yeah? Where does he work then?
Lofty	He was telling me he works from home.

Max	Yeah, well, that's the way of the future, ya know, what with fax machines and computers and modems. They say that one day, leaving home to go to work will be a thing of the past!
Lofty	Seems to me it already is for most of us!
Max	You know what I mean. So, old Steve is working from home as a printer, that's great. The question is, is he doing all right for himself?
Lofty	Phew, just a bit!
Max	Ho! So he's making money is he?
Lofty	Loads of it!
Max	What does he print then?
Lofty	Fives mostly.
Max	Fives? What do you mean, fives?
Lofty	You know, five-pound notes. He reckons the ink is harder to match on tens and twenties.
Max	Wait a minute, are you saying old Steve is working at home printing counterfeit five-pound notes?
Lofty	Well, like he says, there's just no jobs around, is there?
Max	Not even for a really gifted artist like him?
Lofty	Apparently not.
Max	That's incredible! You know, I just can't believe that out of all our group, not one of us has found a proper job! Surely there must be someone?
Lofty	*(Shakes his head as he thinks.)* Well, I can't think of anyone.

Max	What about Biffo? Now there *was* a clever lad. He went to Cambridge, didn't he?
Lofty	Yeah, that's right, he did. I understand he got a first class honours degree as well, in history I think it was.
Max	Blimey! I wonder what he's doing now, I bet he's got a proper job.
Lofty	Antiques dealer.
Max	What?
Lofty	He's an antiques dealer. I see him regularly, he goes into the 'Dog and Gun'.
Max	Well, at least he's done all right for himself!
Lofty	You're kidding! I'd rather be on the dole!
Max	You can't be serious!
Lofty	I am! I'd rather be on the dole than do what he does!
Max	But why? What's wrong with dealing in antiques?
Lofty	Eh?
Max	I said, what's wrong with being an antiques dealer?
Lofty	There's nothing wrong with being an antiques dealer, but I didn't say he was an antiques dealer!
Max	Yes you did! *(Getting annoyed.)* You've just said so, you've just told me he was an antiques dealer!
Lofty	I didn't say that at all. What's the matter with you tonight? *I did not* say he was an antiques dealer!
Max	*(Angrily.)* Look, are you trying to wind me up? You said that he was an antiques dealer, I distinctly heard you say that. *You said that he was an antiques dealer!*

Lofty   *I did not* say he's an antiques dealer!

Max   I'm warning you!

Lofty   It's *you*! You want to get your ears washed out! I said that he's an antiques *stealer*! He doesn't deal in antiques, he *steals* antiques!

Max   Oh.

Lofty   Exactly!

Max   *(After a thoughtful pause.)* Does that mean that none of our group has got a proper job?

Lofty   Nope! Not one!

Max   That's awful! Well if those lads can't get a proper job, what hope have we got? I'm asking ya, what hope is there for *us*?

Lofty   Don't ask me, mate. Who cares about *us* anyway? *(Stands up and takes Max's empty glass.)* Another pint?

GROUP DISCUSSION

Unemployment is a problem with which our society is continually trying to deal and the level of unemployment at any given time is widely viewed as a reliable indicator of the nation's economic health. For this reason, we regularly hear the level of unemployment being discussed, particularly following the release of the latest 'seasonally adjusted figures' on the news.

But unemployment is far more personal than this. For many people, their job is part of their identity: a man might proudly tell you that he is, 'a miner', 'a trawlerman', or a 'bricklayer'. For such a person, being un-employed for any length of time can be devastating, calling into question their worth to society and shattering their self-esteem. For them, unemployment is not 15 per cent, or whatever the current figure is, for them, personally, it is 100 per cent!

For younger people, the problems are different but, if anything, even more severe. Our society now includes a generation of young people a large proportion of whom have known only unemployment. The longer this situation continues, the more difficult it will be for these young people to adapt to a work-orientated lifestyle. It is also under-standable that these young people should feel resentful that society has apparently left them behind.

For this debate, the group is being asked to discuss whether or not it is reasonable to hold the government responsible for the nation's unemployment. Three speakers are to address the group, after which the debate can commence.

Chairperson

Ladies and gentlemen, we are here today to consider the question of unemployment. The issue is, to what extent is it the responsibility of government to ensure adequate employment prospects for the nation?

With this question in mind, we have with us two eminent front-bench politicians who have agreed to address the meeting with their views on this vital issue.

Politician One

Ladies and gentlemen, it is my firmly held view that it is, without a shadow of doubt, the responsibility of government to ensure that those in society who wish to work, are given the opportunity to do so. Let's be quite clear about the role of government. Our government is the managing director of 'Great Britain Limited', the business of our nation, and there is no one else who *can* shoulder this responsibility, there is no one else who can influence the employment market in the way that the government can.

For example, it is the government which has control over public spending. Only the government can boost the construction industry by investing in the nation's roads, building better sea defences, developing the public housing sector, or improving the nation's hospitals and schools.

And, of course, the government is a major employer in its own right and yet, despite the current level of unemployment, we have hospital wards closed because insufficient nurses are employed. Schools are struggling with class sizes that are far too high because insufficient teachers are employed. The police are clearly not coping with crime because insufficient police officers are employed. The list goes on and on and on!

Let's face it, ladies and gentlemen, we, as a nation, are paying for a large proportion of our working population to stay at home while those who do have jobs are working longer hours under an increasing work-load. And, think about it, we are paying building workers to stay at home while our school buildings are a disgrace of disrepair. I really don't see how there can be any doubt about it, unemployment is very definitely an issue for which the government must take full responsibility.

Politician Two

Ladies and gentlemen, what you have just heard does, indeed, have the ring of truth about it, but you must understand that it is a gross over-simplification of the facts. It would be nice to believe that the government could exercise the degree of control necessary to eradicate unemployment, but clearly, this is not the case.

For example, our nation is currently undergoing a technological revolution. Jobs which, a few years ago, were enormously labour intensive, are now carried out by machines. Have you seen how they build cars now? A few computer-controlled robots doing the work of hundreds of men and women and hardly a human worker to be seen on the factory floor. Clearly, this technological revolution is just as fundamental as the industrial revolution was all those years ago and, equally clearly, the government has no control whatsoever over its consequences.

The second point I would like to make is that we are just coming through a recession which has devastated businesses the world over. You only have to look at the ship-building industry, which is now only a shadow of what it was just a few years ago. The government can have no control over such worldwide events and it is naive to suggest otherwise.

Finally, I would like to make the point that even governments do not have endless supplies of money. Yes, we could employ more police officers, school teachers and nurses; yes, we could build new hospitals, schools and council houses; yes, we could spend a fortune on our roads; but where would all this money come from?

Ladies and gentlemen, I am convinced that unemployment is not within the direct control of government and I ask you to confirm that view in your debate.

Crisis in Barcylonica

Copies of the 'Options for Action' list at the end of this sketch will need to be provided for the group. The sketch requires **A servant to King Lipodus**, and two of the king's financial advisers, **Pletimae** and **Volimac**.

Servant to King Lipodus

Ladies and gentlemen, you have been brought here today, as a world-renowned team of experts, to advise King Lipodus of the tiny nation of Barcylonica. The king has asked me to convey to you his deepest gratitude for your help.

As you know, Barcylonica now faces an appalling financial crisis. This has been brought about because several years ago the king accepted funds from international sources to raise the standard of living for his people. He used the money wisely and for the benefit of his people by carrying out the following public works:

1. Two power stations were built providing electricity for homes and factories throughout Barcylonica.
2. A large number of deep boreholes were sunk and clean drinking water was pumped to every community.
3. A new hospital was built in every major town which previously didn't have a hospital.
4. New roads were constructed linking the outlying villages to the towns and thereby to the hospitals.
5. Finally, a small school was built in every village so that every child over the age of five would receive a basic education.

I will now ask the king's financial advisers to explain what went wrong with these wonderful plans for improvement and to describe our options for dealing with the crisis we now face.

Pletimae At first, this programme of improvements was regarded by all as a tremendous success, but soon it became apparent that the interest on the national debt was beyond the country's means. To meet the interest payments demanded, the nation had to raise foreign currency and farmers were told they had to change from growing crops for food to growing crops that could be sold abroad for cash. To achieve this, coffee plantations were created all over the country but soon this meant that food was in short supply and food prices started to go up.

Unfortunately, because of the cold weather this year, the coffee harvest has failed and the nation faces bankruptcy. Despite our very best efforts, we have been unable to find anyone who is able or willing to provide us with the foreign currency we need. In addition, our poorer people are now going hungry.

Volimac The king has only a limited number of means open to him by which he can raise the money needed to meet the interest payments. None of these possible actions is something he would ever do through choice. You have been provided with a list of these options, all of which will raise approximately the same amount of money. What the king requires of you is that you discuss these options and then arrive at an order in which you think they should be employed.

I would suggest that, initially, you each consider the list carefully and make your own individual selection of preferred courses of action. Then you discuss these possible actions as a group and, by democratic means, arrive at your recommended order of priority.

OPTIONS FOR ACTION

A

Close down one of the new power stations. This will mean there would no longer be sufficient electricity for supplying the outlying villages. Without electricity to power the water pumping equipment, this would also mean that people in those villages would no longer have supplies of clean water.

B

Close down 50 per cent of the new hospitals. Most people would still have access to a hospital, but the shortage of beds would mean that only the most urgent cases could be treated.

C

Close down 50 per cent of the village schools. Some of the children affected might be able to travel to nearby schools but the class numbers would then be high and this would mean that the education of all the children would be affected.

D

Ban the use of cars for non-essential use, thereby reducing oil imports. This will only affect the rich and successful, since they are the only people who own cars.

E

Increase the income tax rate to 70 per cent on high wage earners. However, if this *and* item D are employed together, the more successful people will probably leave the kingdom taking their businesses and their wealth with them.

F

Cut income support to single-parent families by 25 per cent. However, because of the shortage of food in the country, many single parents are already finding it extremely difficult to provide for their families.

G

Close the country's only university. Approximately 5 per cent of the country's teenagers are presently offered the opportunity of higher education. Without this university, the prospects for the future of the country would look bleak.

H

Limit the payment of unemployment benefit to a maximum of two years. Approximately 35 per cent of unemployed people would be immediately affected by this and would have all their benefit stopped.

I

Cease all non-essential public services, e.g. close libraries and museums, make street cleaners redundant, cease maintaining parks and public areas.

J

Cut spending on the police force by 20 per cent. Crime is not a major problem in Barcylonica, but there are signs that it may become so, as food runs short.

Mr Dead

A doctor sits at his desk and is scribbling some notes when the next patient arrives. The doctor is self-assured though absent-minded. Initially, the patient is under-confident and hesitant, but this slowly changes to annoyance as the sketch progresses.

Doctor   Yes, come in, take a seat please, Mr . . . er . . . *(glances at his notes)* . . . Mr Dead.

Mr Dear   Thank you, doctor . . . er . . . It's 'Dear'.

Doctor   *(Looking up.)* It's dear? What's dear? I haven't charged you for anything yet!

Mr Dear   *(Tentatively.)* Er . . . My name, doctor. My name's 'Dear', not 'Dead'.

Doctor   Oh! Oh, I see. *(Studies notes closely.)* Yes, it's this handwriting. It's awful, absolutely appalling. I can hardly read it. *(Moves the paper so that it's only inches from his face.)* Actually, it *could* be *my* writing. *(After a pause.)* Makes no difference, I still can't read it! *(Looks up.)* Now then, what seems to be the problem Mr . . . er . . . *(glances at notes.)*

Mr Dear   Dear.

Doctor   Sorry, yes, Mr Dear. Well, what seems to be the problem, Mr Dear?

Mr Dear   I think I have flu. I've had a terribly sore throat, my chest feels heavy and my head's aching all the time.

Doctor   I see. Tell me, Mr . . . er . . . *(glances at notes)* . . . Dead *(then very quickly)* er Dear, are you happy with your life?

Mr Dear   *(Surprised.)* Er . . . no, I don't suppose I am, not at the moment anyway. Work's been difficult lately, I run a business and I've desperately been trying to reduce the noise levels in the factory, it's awful at the moment. Then at home there's the kids – they're both teenagers now, you know – and, well, I suppose you know what teenagers are like! *(Thinks for a moment then shakes his head.)* No, I don't suppose I am very happy with things at the moment, especially with the noise, it's just unbearable!

Doctor   The children are as bad as that, are they?

Mr Dear   No . . . er . . . I was talking about the factory.

Doctor   Oh . . . Right . . . But you *have* been a bit depressed lately?

Mr Dear   Yes, I suppose I have. Do you think that might have something to do with why I feel ill?

Doctor   No, no, not at all, nothing to do with it. It's just that . . . well . . . I wondered if you'd considered euthanasia?

Mr Dear   *(Startled.)* Euthanasia? You mean killing myself?

Doctor   Well, it's not *exactly* killing yourself; in fact, that would be suicide, which is not the same thing at all. No, it would have to be administered by someone like myself, a qualified doctor. I mention it because euthanasia was finally legalised last month and it's now an option which, I suspect, most people don't even consider.

Mr Dear   Er . . . No . . . I don't suppose they do.

Doctor   So, what do you think?

Mr Dear   Well, I'm not *that* unhappy, you understand.

Doctor   It's free!

Mr Dear   Sorry?

Doctor	It's free. I can give it to you on the National Health.
Mr Dear	Well . . . Er . . . No . . . I mean . . . What about my family?
Doctor	You have life insurance, don't you?
Mr Dear	Well, yes, I suppose so.
Doctor	A lot of life insurance?
Mr Dear	Er . . . Yes, quite a bit. My wife and I have always believed in protecting each other in that way.
Doctor	Good, very sensible, Mr . . . er . . . *(glances at notes)*.
Mr Dear	Dear.
Doctor	Sorry?
Mr Dear	Dear. *My name is 'Dear'!*
Doctor	*(Looks at notes.)* Oh, yes, of course. You did tell me didn't you? *(Looks up.)* Yes, as I was saying, very sensible of you to have protected your family with a good life insurance policy and all that. What this means, of course, is that you are now in a position to provide your family with an excellent standard of living.
Mr Dear	I'm not sure I understand!
Doctor	What I'm saying, Mr De . . . De . . . er . . . Dear . . . is that, quite frankly, your family would be better off without you.
Mr Dear	Oh!
Doctor	Yes, clearly for someone in your circumstances, euthanasia would be a very worthwhile option.
Mr Dear	But then I'd be dead!

Doctor	(*Looks at his notes.*) I thought you said your name was 'Dear'?
Mr Dear	(*Angrily.*) My name *is* 'Dear'. What I'm saying is that if I were to choose this euthanasia you keep going on about, I would be dead, deceased, gone, no more!
Doctor	Mmm . . . there is that to it, but then nothing's perfect, you understand. Most treatments have some unwanted side-effect.
Mr Dear	I really don't see how anyone could regard death as being just an unwanted side-effect.
Doctor	Then clearly you don't know much about medicine, Mr . . . er . . . Mr . . . er . . . Oh yes, that's exactly what death is (*almost to himself*), and especially so for surgeons I understand!
Mr Dear	Well, that may be, but I really don't think I'm quite ready for euthanasia yet. If you don't mind I think I'll just settle for some aspirin or something.
Doctor	Well, if that's all you want. It's just that it seems such a waste! These opportunities don't come around every day you know.
Mr Dear	Yes, well, I think some aspirin will do, thank you.
Doctor	Very well, Mr . . . er . . . Mr . . . er . . . Yes, if you're sure that's all you want. It just seems such a shame, such a waste. Oh well, I suppose you'll want a prescription. (*Picks up pen and starts to write. Stops and looks at patient.*) Now what did you say your name was again?

GROUP DISCUSSION

The year is 2010 and euthanasia was legalised two years ago. No specific guidelines were laid down in the legislation except that each individual case must be considered by a committee of lay members (i.e. not medical practitioners) who must decide by a voting majority that euthanasia is appropriate for that particular patient.

Your group is to play the roll of that committee and you are required to debate the following applications submitted by doctors on behalf of their patients.

Case 1

A 32-year-old man who was involved in a motor-cycle accident three years ago. He has never regained consciousness and three doctors have independently agreed that, to all intents and purposes, there is no possibility of recovery.

Case 2

An old lady of 86 who is dying of cancer. The disease has progressed to the point that she has less than two months to live and the strongest pain-killing drugs are no longer effective. The result is that her life has now become intolerable.

Case 3

A child of 3 who is blind, deaf, and mentally retarded to the point that communication in any form is impossible. Three doctors have agreed that there is no hope of any significant improvement.

Case 4

A young man of 24 who broke his neck in a car accident two years ago. He has lost all sensation and movement from the neck down and is unable even to breathe unaided. Three doctors have agreed that there is very little prospect of significant improvement and the young man is so unhappy with what remains of his life that he has specifically requested euthanasia.

Case 5

An old man of 97 who is now senile to the point that he is no longer aware of anything around him. He needs care 24 hours a day and there is no apparent quality to his life. In all other respects his body is healthy.

What Hope Is There for Man?

This sketch requires four people (**A**, **B**, **C** and **D**) who stand in a line facing the audience. Practice will be needed if the rhyme is to flow and, with a sketch like this, it is especially important that the lines are spoken slowly and clearly.

A   We come here from the future,
        a world you've not yet seen.

B   From where the sky is purple,
        and clouds are mottled green.

C   Where creatures all are mutants,
        and cats don't miaow, they bark.

D   Where street-lights just aren't needed,
        'cause things glow in the dark!

A   And we have come to beg you,
        to do the best you can.

B   If you don't save this planet,
        what hope is there for man?

C   Don't leave it till tomorrow,
        you really mustn't wait.

D   We come from your tomorrow,
        tomorrow's much too late!

A   Yes we came from your future,
to tell how it will be.

B   To show how you're destroying,
the land, the air, the sea.

C   And you must now consider,
there is a price to pay.

D   For you to save tomorrow,
the world must change today.

A   Your factories spew out toxins,
pollution fills the air,

B   And filthy hydrocarbons,
are choking everywhere.

C   And all those cfc's,
the ozone will deplete.

D   That's all that stands between us,
and life-destroying heat!

A   They're chopping down the forests,
for all that they are worth.

B   Yes burning and destroying,
the lungs of Mother Earth.

C   They've cut and burned whole countries,
vast acres at a go.

D   They're trading life-filled forests,
for land where crops won't grow.

A   Those people there are hungry,
and trees can't help it's true.

B   But you have wealth and power,
and so it's up to you!

C   Please help them feed their people,
provide the food they need.

D   The Earth has food in plenty,
but not enough for greed.

A   And seas and oceans plundered,
fished bare for fishing's sake.

B   They've taken every species,
till nothing's left to take.

C   They've squandered those resources,
fish killed and thrown away.

D   Or made to fertiliser,
a debt the future'll pay.

A   And now we have to leave you,
the future calls us home.

B   A strange and dying planet,
not like the Earth you roam.

C   This future waits tomorrow,
if you don't make a plan.

D   What chances for our planet?
What hope is there for man?

GROUP DISCUSSION

Everywhere we look, the Earth is being damaged by people who place their immediate wants and needs above all else. Realistically, what hope do we have of changing this selfish attitude on a worldwide scale? Perhaps more importantly, what hope is there for future generations if we don't?

But to change the world requires some difficult decisions, choices which are far from clear cut. Action taken to protect the environment in one way may cause further damage in another, in the same way that, for example, the building of new sea defences in one region may result in even greater erosion further down the coast where the beach is no longer replenished.

You are the elected councillors of the large and busy market town of Choak, in Southern Ireland. Over recent years, air pollution has become a major problem for the town, so much so, in fact, that the town is now usually referred to as Choak-in-Eire.

In order to rectify the situation, the town council has prepared a list of proposals which it hopes will bring about an improvement in the air quality in the town centre. This list has been publicised and comments invited from interested parties. The proposals and the comments which they attracted are listed below and you, as the town council, are required to discuss the arguments before voting on whether the proposals should be implemented or abandoned.

Choak-in-Eire Town Council
Proposed Town Centre Improvements

Proposals

1. To exclude all cars from the town centre.
2. To pedestrianise the town centre.
3. To impose strictly enforced pollution limits on all factories within five miles of the town.
4. To prohibit the burning of peat on all household fires.

Comments Received

1. The Local Clean Air Action Group

a. The banning of cars from the centre of the town will bring about a substantial improvement in the quality of the air in the town centre and we fully support this measure.

b. However, if, as a result of this measure, shoppers desert the town in favour of the newly opened, out-of-town retail parks, the resulting extra use of cars will greatly increase the over-all level of air pollution.

c. The imposition of strict pollution controls on industry within the region of the town can only improve the situation and is welcomed.

d. Prohibiting the burning of peat on domestic fires would, at first glance, reduce the level of pollution in the town. However, the peat is a local resource which is excavated efficiently and which requires little in the way of transportation. It must be recognised, therefore, that any change to a smokeless fuel will involve considerable long-distance haulage in order to import sufficient quantities of suitable fuels. This would have consequences in terms of air and noise pollution from heavy goods vehicles.

2. The Local Shopkeepers Action Group

a. Banning cars from the town centre will bring about the death of the town. Experience in other towns has shown that shoppers will not abandon their cars and will simply go elsewhere.

b. With the town centre shops already suffering from the competition of the new out-of-town retail parks, it is unlikely that many town shops would survive and the town would become a boarded-up ghost town of 'TO LET' and 'FOR SALE' signs.

c. With cars no longer allowed in the town centre, all the garages and petrol stations in the town would close. The redevelopment of these sites would be extremely expensive (and, therefore, unlikely in the near future) because of the cost of dealing with the large underground petrol storage tanks. These boarded-up garages would further add to the impression of desolation in the town.

3. Local Chamber of Commerce

a. The Chamber has mixed feelings on the pedestrianisation of the town centre. This scheme could be a success if the town centre were made attractive enough to persuade the shoppers to use the 'park and ride' public transport system. However, if the shoppers chose to take their trade elsewhere, the town centre would become a disaster zone. It is important to recognise that if large numbers of shops start to close, it would be almost impossible to reverse the process. With a lot of shops closed, people will stop using the town: without customers, the remaining shops will quickly close.

b. The imposition of strict pollution limits on the town's factories will be disastrous for the companies involved and, in turn, for employment in the region. The companies concerned will be faced with the enormous cost of modifying their factories and will see their production costs soar compared with competitors located elsewhere. Needless to say, many factories will close and thousands of jobs will be lost from the region.

Cardboard City

Our two friends, **Max** and **Lofty**, are once again chatting in the local pub.

Lofty   I haven't seen you for a few days, Max, you been ill?

Max   Naw, been down to the Old Smoke, mate.

Lofty   Down to the old smoke? What do ya mean? Ere, you haven't taken up cigarettes or something daft like that have ya?

Max   Naw, nothing like that, Lofty, me old pal. I've been down to London. That's what they call London, ya know, the Old Smoke!

Lofty   I didn't know that. Interesting that.

Max   I tell ya, there's some sights to be seen down there, Lofty, there really is!

Lofty   Ya mean like the Beefeaters n' that?

Max   Beefeaters? Naw, I didn't go to any burger bars. Where would I get the money to go to burger bars?

Lofty   Beefeaters aren't burger bars, they're the guards for the Tower of London!

Max   Oh!

Lofty   So what were you doing in London, then?

Max   Oh, it was awful. I saw some homeless kids living on the streets. They were sleeping in cardboard boxes! One of 'em was barely in his teens and I saw him eating food out of a rubbish bin! It was really awful!

Lofty   A tourist, eh?

Max	Don't be daft, he'd run away from home! That's how most of 'em end up on the streets.
Lofty	I meant *you*! *You* were a tourist!
Max	Me? Oh, yeah, I suppose I was. I stayed with an uncle of mine who lives in a real poor area on the outskirts of the city. The houses are all run down and most of the people who live there are out of work.
Lofty	Yeah? *(Shakes his head.)* But it's not good enough really, is it? I mean, no one should be allowed to live in such appalling conditions, should they? Something ought to be done about it!
Max	*(Offended.)* Well, it wasn't as bad as all that! It's a lovely little house inside, comfortable as you could want and as clean as anything. He's even got double glazing! *(Almost to himself.)* Though I don't know why he bought double glazing at his age!
Lofty	I was talking about those homeless kids you saw!
Max	Oh! Yeah, that's all wrong. Something should be done about it! The politicians should get their heads together and sort it out.
Lofty	Yeah, you're right there, Max, me old mate. *(After a brief pause.)* Of course it's the salesmen I blame.
Max	The salesmen! Why the salesmen? What have they got to do with homeless kids in London?
Lofty	I wasn't talking about the homeless kids in London, I was talking about your uncle's double glazing! I meant that some salesmen'll sell anything to anyone as long as they get commission!
Max	Oh, yeah, I see what ya mean. It's sad 'cause old people are always vulnerable; they can be so gullible can't they?

Lofty	*(Sips his beer, after a pause.)* You're dead right in what you said though, something ought to be done about it. I'd bang their heads together, me!
Max	The old people?
Lofty	Don't be daft! Why would I want to do that?
Max	Oh, you mean the salesmen!
Lofty	Naw, I'm talking about the politicians. You said they should get their heads together, I'm saying I'd like to bang their heads together! They should do something to help those homeless kids.
Max	Politicians? They're so full of promises in the run up to elections, then the rest of the time they don't give a damn about ordinary people!
Lofty	It sounds like they need all the help they can get!
Max	The politicians? Why do they need help?
Lofty	Not the politicians, the homeless kids!
Max	Oh, I was gonna say! The politicians don't need any help, if anyone knows how to look after themselves, they do. I bet they can have just about anything they want, I bet they have a life of luxury.
Lofty	I wonder what they eat?
Max	Humph! Anything they want! I bet they go to the best restaurants and don't even look at the prices before they go in!
Lofty	Eh?
Max	The politicians, I bet they don't even look at the prices before they go into a restaurant!
Lofty	I was talking about the homeless kids! Will you stop going on about politicians!

Max	Oh, sorry.
Lofty	I was wondering what the homeless kids find to eat in rubbish bins.
Max	Well, they say that there's no shortage of food in the rubbish bins of London. Someone once told me you could feed most of Africa with the food they throw away from the restaurants in London!
Lofty	It's no way to live though, is it?
Max	(*Shakes his head.*) Naa, it is not. I tell ya, if the politicians' kids were sleeping in cardboard boxes and eating food out of rubbish bins, the problem would be sorted out within a week.
Lofty	Do you know, I'd never thought about that! That's incredible, what you just said!
Max	You bet your life it is, flaming politicians!
Lofty	Look, I wasn't talking about the politicians, will you stop going on about politicians! I was talking about the food in the rubbish bins, what you just said about there being enough food in the rubbish bins of London's restaurants to feed most of Africa. Do you know, I bet it's just about true as well!
Max	Yeah, there's something very wrong with the way we run this world, isn't there?
Lofty	Yeah, but what can we do about it?
Max	Nothing, mate, nothing at all. Ya see, it's all down to power. Those at the top of the pile always have the first bite of the cherry. Unfortunately, there's never enough left for those at the bottom. It's the same the whole world over. The street kids and down n' outs have no power at all, not even voting power.
Lofty	Yeah, I suppose you're right. After all, if anyone *really* cared, they'd have done something about it!

GROUP DISCUSSION

The small South Pacific island of Wairarwe, which is still not shown on the latest maps of the Pacific Basin, has recently suffered a dramatic reduction in its income from tourism. (This is primarily because the cruise-liner, *Sea Jaded*, which has traditionally made Wairarwe a port of call, has been unable to find the island since the old captain retired.)

As a consequence of this, the tribal elders are meeting to review their public spending plans for the coming year and have decided to reduce public spending from 93 million Nhows to 76 million Nhows. (The current exchange rate is roughly 1.6 Pounds Stirling equals one Wairarwe Nhow.)

The public spending budget of the Wairarwe elders is shared between the six sub-sections of the Department of Social Security, Education, Retirement and Sickness (DOSSERS), a department renowned for their short working hours (each hour is only 40 minutes) and long holidays.

The group is to play the part of the Wairarwe elders and should start the meeting by examining the table below which outlines the costs of maintaining the services provided by the DOSSERS. The purpose of the meeting is to discuss how the 76 million Nhows available for the coming year should be spent on the public services outlined and then to reach agreement on the allocation of funds.

Department of Social Security, Education, Retirement and Sickness

Costs of Maintaining Services

SUB-SECTION 1: THE HOMELESS

Option 1
All young homeless people will be accommodated in modern houses (maximum 7 people per house) each to receive training and assistance until suitable employment has been found.
Cost 8,000,000 Nhows

Option 2
As above but no funds available for training or assistance.
Cost 7,000,000 Nhows

Option 3
All young homeless people to be accommodated in hostels of up to 100 people.
Cost 5,000,000 Nhows

SUB-SECTION 2: THE UNEMPLOYED

Option 1
Unemployed people will receive sufficient benefit for a good standard of living.
Cost 25,000,000 Nhows

Option 2
Unemployed people will receive sufficient benefit for a basic standard of living.
Cost 22,000,000 Nhows

Option 3
Unemployed people will receive sufficient benefit for a basic standard of living but for a maximum of two years only.
Cost 18,000,000 Nhows

SUB-SECTION 3: THE DISABLED

Option 1
Disabled people to receive a good living allowance and to be provided with specially equipped homes and cars.
Cost 10,000,000 Nhows

Option 2
As above but cars will not be available.
Cost 8,000,000 Nhows

Option 3
Disabled people will receive a living allowance only.
Cost 6,000,000 Nhows

SUB-SECTION 4: THE ELDERLY

Option 1
Elderly people to receive a high standard of care with regular outings and a Christmas bonus.
Cost 13,000,000 Nhows

Option 2
As above but without the outings and Christmas bonus.
Cost 11,000,000 Nhows

Option 3
Elderly people to receive basic care only.
Cost 9,000,000 Nhows

SUB-SECTION 5: ONE-PARENT FAMILIES

Option 1
Individual houses to be provided for all one-parent families together with a good living allowance.
Cost 17,000,000 Nhows

Option 2
As above but with only a basic living allowance.
Cost 15,000,000 Nhows

Option 3
Group accommodation to be provided for all one-parent families together with a basic living allowance.
Cost 13,000,000 Nhows

SUB-SECTION 6: EDUCATION

Option 1
Education available free to everyone under 21 years of age.
Cost 20,000,000 Nhows

Option 2
Education available free to everyone under 17 years of age.
Cost 17,000,000 Nhows

Option 3
Education available free to children under 12 only.
Cost 15,000,000 Nhows

Total Cost of Ideal Solutions

Option 1
93,000,000 Nhows

Total Cost of Compromise Solutions

Option 2
80,000,000 Nhows

Total Cost of Minimum Provision

Option 3
66,000,000 Nhows

Total funds available 76,000,000 Nhows

Mercy Mission

This sketch requires four people: a narrator, a doctor, a charity representative, and a civil engineer. They address the rest of the group in turn, being as persuasive as possible.

Narrator   Ladies and gentlemen, the province of Kamchenka, in the small country of Mulgravia, located in the southern hemisphere, suffered an earthquake – measuring 7.2 on the Richter Scale – in the early hours of this morning. First reports indicate that there has been extensive and widespread damage and many of the buildings in the capital city and the surrounding towns have suffered partial or total collapse.

It is too early for reliable reports of the numbers of people killed or injured, but the reports of extensive damage to property suggest that the number of casualties is likely to be high.

This earthquake has stuck Mulgravia at the very worst possible time, at the very onset of the season when the country will be racked by wave after wave of tropical storms. This will make the rescue of those trapped in collapsed buildings particularly difficult and supplies of humanitarian aid will be limited by the problems of landing and unloading aircraft on the tiny Mulgravian airstrip under such extreme weather conditions.

The weather forecast for the region suggests that there is the possibility of landing one aircraft prior to the arrival of the first storm. Relief supplies are being loaded onto this aircraft at this very moment and it has been brought to our attention that there is space for one extra person in addition to the flight crew.

Ladies and gentlemen, you have been selected, as good and decent citizens, to make a choice which will be difficult by any standards. Your roll is to select one of the three experts who are with us tonight, to be allocated the seat on this aircraft. You will need to choose between a doctor, a charity representative and a civil engineer. Please make your choice carefully, since this may be the only opportunity to send expert help to Mulgravia for some weeks, which is a long time in these circumstances. The lives of thousands of men, women, and children could depend on your choice.

Doctor Ladies and gentlemen, I am a doctor specialising in tropical medicine and during my time working abroad I have also gained extensive experience of dealing with the after-effects of earthquakes.

There are a number of immediate medical problems which face the people of Mulgravia. The first of these is the physical injuries which perhaps thousands of people will have suffered in the collapsed buildings and as a result of masonry from buildings falling into the streets. Many of the injuries suffered will be crush injuries, therefore, which require a particular form of treatment. I am well qualified to work with the medical professionals in Mulgravia to speed up the treatment of those injured using the latest techniques. I am confident that my presence in Mulgravia will reduce the suffering and save the lives of many of those who have received physical injuries in the earthquake.

In countries such as Mulgravia, which do not have the substantial resources necessary to build towns and cities resistant to earthquakes, there will be a number of secondary health problems. Primarily, these will stem from the damage caused to the drinking water and sewerage systems during the earthquake. Water mains and sewer pipes will have been fractured in hundreds of locations, with the result that very few areas will still have a water supply. Where supplies do exist, they will almost certainly be contaminated. This is likely to lead to the onset of a number of extremely serious diseases. Unchecked, these diseases will quickly become epidemics and I would regard it as one of my main responsibilities to ensure this did not happen.

Ladies and gentlemen, you will shortly hear from a charity representative and from a civil engineer, both of whom will claim that they can achieve considerably more than I can. However, I ask you to remember that the people of Mulgravia desperately need immediate medical assistance and only I am able to provide that assistance. There is a place for me on the aircraft; please do not allow innocent lives to be lost by refusing me that place.

Thank you for giving me your attention.

Charity Manager

Ladies and gentlemen, the people of Mulgravia need a very great deal of help, far more than any one man can hope to provide, even if he is a well-qualified and very experienced doctor or civil engineer.

The people of Mulgravia will have a large number of very urgent needs. Yes, medical assistance, vaccinations and drugs will be an urgent requirement, but so too will food and a supply of wholesome drinking water. In addition, it is likely that many people will find themselves without roofs over their heads and I'm sure I don't need to describe to you what that will mean in a country which will soon be subject to a series of tropical storms!

Yes, the people of Mulgravia are in very desperate need of help on a massive scale. Only the largest charity organisations are geared up for coping with such disasters and for providing the supplies and assistance needed.

Ladies and gentlemen, I am a representative of several of the world's largest charities. I admit that I am not qualified to offer immediate medical assistance to the injured and dying, but I am qualified to assess the needs of the people of Mulgravia and I am empowered to mobilise the disaster relief teams of the world's leading charities. This, I promise you, will happen just as soon as the storms abate sufficiently for mercy missions to commence.

I accept that if you send me on that aircraft instead of the doctor who has just addressed you, a few lives may indeed be lost as a consequence. However, in the longer term, I believe that you will be better serving the needs of the Mulgravian people and I am confident that time will prove that many more people will have been saved.

Thank you, ladies and gentlemen, for giving me your time.

Civil Engineer

Ladies and gentlemen, I am a qualified civil engineer and I have spent my life helping communities and countries recover from earthquakes.

The damage that will have been caused in Mulgravia by an earthquake of a magnitude of 7.2 will be catastrophic! Bridges and fly-overs will have been destroyed, tunnels will have collapsed, roads will be impassable, the region's railways will be inoperative. In short, the transport of people and the haulage of goods in that region of Mulgravia will be virtually impossible. Just think what that means for the two others who are offering to assist the people there. The doctor will be restricted to working in one hospital because he will find it impossible to travel around the region. He will also find that he has very few patients to treat, simply because there will be no way of getting them to hospital.

Similarly, the charity representative will find it impossible to assess the needs of the Mulgravian people accurately, simply because he will be unable to visit the areas worst hit by the earthquake! He will be reduced to guessing the needs of the people, something which I am quite sure he could do here and now, without taking that valuable place on the aircraft.

But let's examine further the damage that will have

been caused by that earthquake. As has already been mentioned, water mains and sewerage pipes will have been extensively damaged. In addition, telephone systems will certainly not be operational, power supplies will be down, and thousands of buildings will be damaged and will urgently need to be made safe.

Ladies and gentlemen, what is urgently needed in Mulgravia is a civil engineer with earthquake experience. I am that person and if you allocate the seat on that aircraft to me, I will work to restore supplies of clean drinking water, I will organise repairs to the roads and railways so that food can be distributed once it has been air-lifted in, and I will organise teams of men to make the damaged buildings safe so that more people are not injured by falling masonry.

Ladies and gentlemen, I ask you to allocate the seat on that aircraft to me.

Doctor   Ladies and gentlemen, I urge you to think this through! What can one civil engineer really achieve in the face of such widespread damage? Please, please, remember I *can* save lives if you will allow me.

Narrator   Well, I'm afraid I must stop your presentations there. Time is running out and we must now decide who is to be allocated that seat on the aircraft. What I would like you to do, ladies and gentlemen, is to discuss what you think can be achieved by each of the three experts and then decide, by taking a vote, who is to be allocated that seat.

Rough Justice

This sketch requires two plain-clothes police officers and a motorist. The motorist is being interviewed in the police station and is seated facing the audience with a police officer standing on either side of him/her. The police officers are deliberately intimidating the motorist who is clearly worried. Since the police officers are almost taking it in turns to speak, the motorist is continually turning his head from side to side in order to face the officer speaking.

Officer 1   Right then, sir, I'm Chief Inspector Brian Dee, known around here as C.I. Dee of the C.I.D. *(He chuckles and then indicates the other police officer.)* And this is Detective Inspector Joseph King.

Officer 2   *(Leans over the prisoner in an intimidating manner.)* Some people think my name's a funny name, sir, and they come up to me and they say, 'You must be Joe-King!' *(Pause.)* I think it's only fair to warn you, sir, that I don't find that funny at all, in fact, it makes me very angry! *(Moves closer to intimidate the prisoner.)* Believe me, sir, you wouldn't like me when I'm angry!

Officer 1   Now then, sir, would you like to tell us *your* name?

Prisoner   Er . . . S . . Smith, officer. S . . S . . Simon Smith.

Officer 2   Right, Mr Smith, would you care to explain to us exactly what it was you were doing when you were arrested?

Prisoner   Nothing! I was doing nothing!

Officer 1   Nothing, sir? You must have been doing *something*!

Prisoner   No! I mean yes! I mean, I was doing nothing wrong!

Officer 2   Are you accusing us of unlawful arrest, sir? That's a very serious accusation.

Prisoner   No! No! N . . Not at all! But there must be some mistake! *(Turns to Officer 1 expecting the next question to come from that direction but Officer 2 speaks again.)*

Officer 2   Well if you weren't doing anything wrong, sir, you won't mind telling us what you were doing.

Prisoner   Well, I'd just been into the post office to buy some stamps and when I came out, you were there waiting for me.

Officer 1   So tell me, sir, why do you think you've been arrested?

Prisoner   I don't know, I just don't know! I keep telling you there must have been some mistake!

Officer 2   You're not suggesting we've made a mistake, are you, sir?

Prisoner   No! I mean yes! I mean I just don't understand what I've done wrong. All I did was to buy some postage stamps!

Officer 1   Yesss . . But while you were busy buying postage stamps, sir, where was your car?

Prisoner   *(Surprised.)* My car? Just in front of the post office. I'd just pulled to the side of the road for a moment while I ran into the post office.

Officer 2   Exactly! And did you notice some funny yellow stripes painted at the side of the road at that point, sir?

Prisoner   Sorry?

Officer 1   Did you notice the double yellow lines where you parked, sir?

Prisoner   Oh! Yes, I see what you're getting at!

Officer 2   So you *did* notice the yellow lines?

Prisoner   (*Relaxing.*) Yes, OK, so I parked on double yellow lines for a minute or so. Surely you haven't brought me here just because of that!

Officer 1   Make a note of that Detective Inspector. Mr Smith admits the offence.

Prisoner   Yeah, OK, I admit that I parked on double yellow lines. Now, would you mind just giving me a ticket and letting me go? I've an important meeting this afternoon.

Officer 1   This is a very serious offence, sir.

Prisoner   Parking on double yellow lines, you must be joking!

Officer 2   No, sir, I'm Joe King and I told you I get very angry when people say that.

Prisoner   Look, you're not intimidating me any more. You can't just arrest me and treat me like this, not just for parking on double yellow lines. I know my rights!

Officer 2   Do you, sir? Then you'll know all about the 'Public Safety Act' which was passed last month, do you, sir?

Prisoner   Er . . .

Officer 1   The Act which states that anybody found guilty of wilfully endangering the life of a member of the public, shall be hanged by the neck until dead!

Prisoner   You must be joke . . . (*He turns apprehensively to Officer 2 as he realises what he is saying.*)

Officer 2   (*Glaring at the prisoner who stops mid-sentence.*) Yes, sir, that's exactly what the Act requires, but you mustn't worry. I mean, you'll almost certainly spend the rest of your life in prison, but at least it won't be a long sentence!

Prisoner	You can't be serious! I was only parked on double yellow lines for a minute! How can that merit the death penalty? You must both be mad! How can parking on double yellow lines endanger anybody's life?
Officer 1	And what if a fire engine couldn't get through to fight a fire?
Officer 2	Or an ambulance?
Officer 1	Or what if a child had stepped out from behind your illegally parked car and been knocked over?
Prisoner	Well, I hardly think . . .
Officer 2	Have you seen a newspaper today, sir?
Prisoner	No, not yet.
Officer 1	Then you haven't heard that a motorist was hanged yesterday for doing 40 miles per hour in a built-up area?
Prisoner	You must be joke . . . I don't believe it!
Officer 2	It's true, sir. It's a very useful piece of legislation, the Public Safety Act. Far more effective than the Road Traffic Act ever was. (*Shakes his head.*) Penalty points on driving licences never were much of a deterrent.
Officer 1	Yes, just think about it, sir. Within the next couple of weeks there will have been a hanging for exceeding the speed limit (*holds up his hand and counts on his fingers*) and a hanging for illegal parking. I'm telling you, the standard of driving in this country will improve dramatically over the next few weeks, you just wait and see.
Officer 2	(*To Officer 1.*) Well, I hardly think he can wait and see, C.I. Dee. How can he wait and see?
Officer 1	Oh yeah! I hadn't thought of that! (*Laughs and turns*

to the Prisoner.) Of course you won't be able to wait and see, will you sir? *(Laughs and nudges Prisoner with his elbow as if sharing a good joke.)* You'll be dead won't you?!

Prisoner   Look! I don't believe a word of this. You're just trying to frighten me. I demand to see a lawyer!

Officer 2   A lawyer, sir? You'll never find a lawyer to defend you on this one, sir!

Prisoner   I don't know what you're both up to but I want to speak to a lawyer now!

Officer 1   I'm afraid he's right, sir, you won't find a lawyer who's willing to defend you on a charge under the Public Safety Act.

Prisoner   And why not?!

Officer 1   Because if a lawyer were to get you off, and then you went out in your car and killed a child, under the new Act, that child's death would be the lawyer's fault! That means *he'd* be facing the death penalty!

Prisoner   Look, you can't just go executing people like that. Human life is very precious, you can't just destroy it as if it had no value!

Officer 1   That's a strange notion you have, sir, that human life is precious. I don't know where you got that idea from. It seems to me that the exact opposite is true, that there's far too many people in the world. If that's the case, the best thing we can do is to get rid of the people who don't live by society's rules. Believe me, the world will be a better place for it!

Officer 2   Absolutely right, C.I. Dee. *(Then to the prisoner.)* Where in heaven did you get this idea that life is precious? Who's been going around saying that people are important?

GROUP DISCUSSION

For Christians, the suggestion that human life has no value is fundamentally abhorrent, but for atheists there is a logic to the police officer's argument. Our society continually struggles to cope with those of its members who cannot or will not live by its rules and the lives of good, law-abiding citizens are frequently devastated by their illegal activities. Capital punishment would be an inexpensive solution to this problem and an excellent deterrent to others – would *you* continue to park on double yellow lines if . . . ?

This is an extreme argument, but even some Christians continue to believe that there is justification for reinstating the death penalty for one or more specified crimes.

What does the group believe? Is it possible for the group to reach unanimous agreement on any of the following propositions?

A

Capital punishment cannot be justified under any circumstances.

B

Capital punishment should be reinstated for certain specified crimes, perhaps including one or more of the following:

1. Mass murder.

2. Repeated offences which involve extreme violence.

3. Repeated sexual offences against children.

4. Repeated violent or sexual offences against anyone.

5. Repeated offences involving the distribution of drugs to very young children.

6. Murder of a policeman.

7. Treason.

8. Terrorism.

9. Others . . . ?

C

Capital punishment should be reinstated for anyone who repeatedly demonstrates that he or she is unable to live within the rules of society to the extent that they are a permanent danger to society.

But this issue raises a further important question for Christians. Jesus tells us that we should not judge. How could our society survive if no one was prepared to judge the innocence or guilt of others? Does this mean that a wholly Christian society would be unworkable? (Even Christians break the law!) What views does the group have on this? Do they see a difference between judging people against the rules of society and judging people against our personal interpretation of Christian standards?

Who Can You Trust?

A Member of Parliament has been invited on to a talk-show to discuss MPs' salaries and their 'outside interests'. The sketch calls for two people, the **Interviewer** and **Mr Safeseat**.

Interviewer *(To the audience.)* Good evening, ladies and gentlemen. I am very pleased to welcome tonight a well-known Member of Parliament who has recently had to face the two thorny questions of MPs' pay and of Members having to declare their outside interests. With me tonight, then, is the renowned Member of Parliament, the well-known back-bencher, Ivor Safeseat. *(Turns to Mr Safeseat.)* If I can start by asking you, Mr Safeseat, what are your thoughts on the recent debate on MPs' pay?

Mr Safeseat *(Condescendingly.)* Well, quite honestly, David, no one would go into politics nowadays for the money, there's far more money to be made in industry. No, people enter politics because they feel the need to serve society, because they feel they have something to contribute to the country and because they want to work for the greater good of our people. Indeed, personally, I find the opportunity to serve – and the knowledge of a job well done – is sufficient reward in itself.

Interviewer So you're against the proposed pay increase?

Mr Safeseat Now, I didn't say that, David. You really must try not to put words into my mouth.

Interviewer I'm sorry, it's just that you said . . .

Mr Safeseat *(Interrupting.)* No, no, no, not at all, don't apologise! You see, while I personally find that serving one's country is sufficient reward in itself, I also recognise the need for us to attract to Parliament people of the very highest calibre. Obviously, that is only going to be possible if we pay good salaries.

Interviewer Yes, but MPs' pay is already very high!

Mr Safeseat Not compared to the leaders of industry! Surely our country deserves a management team at least as good as that in industry?

Interviewer Yes, I suppose, put like that . . . *(Looks at his notes.)* And, of course, the House has also recently faced the difficult question of Members having to declare their outside interests.

Mr Safeseat Difficult? Why do you say difficult? I can assure you that we have absolutely nothing to hide!

Interviewer But I understand that, like many MP's, you hold a number of directorships for which you receive substantial additional earnings?

Mr Safeseat *(Laughs.)* You don't want to believe everything you read in the press, you know, David!

Interviewer Oh! So you don't hold any directorships?

Mr Safeseat Now, I didn't say that! There you go putting words into my mouth again! *(Shrugs.)* Naturally, I want to do everything I can to contribute to the prosperity of this wonderful country and if I can help in some small way by offering advice to one or two of our most distinguished firms, of course I'm only too pleased to be able to do so.

Interviewer So how many companies exactly do you advise in this way?

Mr Safeseat Oh, I couldn't say exactly. A few.

Interviewer Quite frankly, Mr Safeseat, I am led to believe that it's more than just a few! In fact, I am told that you hold something like 138 directorships!

Mr Safeseat Nonsense! Where on earth did you hear that!?

Interviewer From one of your colleagues actually!

Mr Safeseat Well I can assure you that he's misinformed; it's nothing like 138!

Interviewer Well, if you'd like to set the record straight, Mr Safeseat, how many directorships do you in fact hold?

Mr Safeseat I couldn't say exactly.

Interviewer Approximately then.

Mr Safeseat I really couldn't say!

Interviewer So 138 could be correct then?

Mr Safeseat Definitely not! Nowhere near that number! Certainly no more than 136.

Interviewer Even 136 seems an awful lot of directorships!

Mr Safeseat Yes, I can see that it might seem that way to the uninformed, but you can understand, I'm sure, that when British companies approach me for help, it would be nothing short of unpatriotic for me to turn them away.

Interviewer *(Sceptically.)* Yes . . ., quite. *(Glances at his notes.)* I think I read – please correct me if I'm wrong – that your declared earnings from these directorships is something like £600,000 per year!

Mr Safeseat It may be something like that, I couldn't say for sure, the money's not important!

Interviewer But you accept, I assume, that to the ordinary working man £600,000 a year is nothing short of a fortune!

Mr Safeseat *(Shakes his head and then continues patiently.)* All through my political career I've made it clear that I will do everything in my power to build up this great nation of ours. I am happy to tell you that supporting British industry is just one of the many ways that I have worked – tirelessly and ceaselessly I might add – for the good of our country. If one or two of those companies feel that my contribution to their success, and to the success of our nation, deserves recognition in some small way, then I am pleased to accept that token of their gratitude in all humility.

Interviewer   Yes, but £600,000 a year!

Mr Safeseat   Those are your figures, not mine!

Interviewer   Then tell us what the correct figure is.

Mr Safeseat   Now, David, if I could, I would. I honestly don't know. As I have said already, the money is not important. It could easily be less than the figure you have quoted!

Interviewer   Or even more?

Mr Safeseat   There you go putting words into my mouth again! Honestly, I really can't say. But come on, David, you have known me long enough to know that I believe in totally honest government, everything out in the open and above board, nothing hidden away, nothing festering out of sight!

Interviewer   But Mr Safeseat, I was given to understand that you voted against Members having to declare their outside interests?

Mr Safeseat   Yes, but purely because I don't think it serves the common good one jot for the gutter press – and I don't include you in that term you understand – as I was saying, for the gutter press to go raking about for any titbits that they can use to slander the names of perfectly good and decent Members of Parliament.

Interviewer   And you don't believe that your having all those directorships in any way influences your work in Parliament?

Mr Safeseat   Good gracious, no. As I said right at the beginning, no one would go into politics for the money. Members of Parliament exist just to serve and the people know they can trust us to put their interests above all other considerations! But let me put it another way – if you can't trust your own elected Member of Parliament, *who can you trust?*

GROUP DISCUSSION

This sketch has a political content which you may or may not be happy with; that is how it should be, Christians cannot expect to agree with each other on everything. (They should, however, try to be more tolerant of the views of others!)

The main question raised by this sketch, though, is one of trust, just how far *can* we trust those people who are supposed to represent our interests: politicians, civil servants, the police, doctors, etc.? Mr Safeseat is clearly willing to explain and justify his actions, but that doesn't mean his *real* motives are beyond reproach.

In all walks of life, people are faced with moral dilemmas. For example, the perfectly legitimate wish of a Member of Parliament to provide his family with a good standard of living becomes a 'thorny question' when Members of Parliament are responsible for setting their own salaries (salaries which are, of course, paid out of taxpayers' money!)

Consider the following pairs of comments. In each case, the views expressed are extreme and your own view will almost certainly lie somewhere between the two. Discuss the extreme views quoted and share your own views with the group if you feel able. Do you have any personal experience of a 'caring professional' who has betrayed your trust?

1. 'Doctors have dedicated their lives to the service of the community through medicine. I trust my doctor implicitly.'

'Doctors today are only concerned with minimising their work-load and maximising the profitability of their practices. Patients needing a great deal of care are now passed from practice to practice and patients now are only referred to costly specialists as a last resort.'

2. 'The British police force is the best in the world and we can be justifiably proud of it. I think it is wonderful that so many men and women are prepared to place their own lives in jeopardy to defend all that is good in our society. I believe the integrity of the police is beyond question and I would trust them without reservation.'

'The British police force has been shown to be corrupt time after time. Innocent people have suffered years of wrongful imprisonment because of the deliberate falsifying of evidence – and for no better reason than that public opinion demanded a conviction! I wouldn't trust the police at all!'

3. 'Our vicar is a wonderful man, without doubt a man of God. I trust him 110 per cent!'

'I think vicars are no better than the rest of us; if anything, they're worse! Every time you pick up a newspaper you read about some vicar who's run off with someone else's wife or who's been paying too much attention to the choir boys! I wouldn't trust one as far as I could throw one!'

The truth is, of course, we are all human and, therefore, all fallible. None of us is perfect and part of the process of acquiring 'an old head' (you know, that strange thing never found on young shoulders) is learning to watch out for the little clues which indicate whether someone is likely to be trustworthy. As Jesus said, 'Whoever can be trusted with very little can also be trusted with much, and whoever is dishonest with very little will also be dishonest with much.' *(Luke 16:10)*

Choices

This sketch calls for two young people, a boy and a girl, each wearing a rolled-up paper unicorn horn on their head. The girl stands centre stage, manicuring her nails. The boy enters waving his arms in exasperation.

Boy   I don't believe it! I just don't believe it!

Girl   *(Unperturbed, continues to examine her nails.)* What's the matter now, dear? What on earth has upset you?

Boy   It's that man, you know, Noah! I'm telling you, he is definitely a sandwich short of a picnic!

Girl   *(Without looking up.)* You mean that Noah who is building that enormous house on the hill?

Boy   That's just the point! Apparently it isn't a house he's building at all, it's a boat!

Girl   *(Still not looking up, continues to examine her nails.)* A boat, dear? Oh, I wouldn't have thought so. Where on earth could he sail a great boat like that round here? I mean, we're miles from the sea, aren't we?

Boy   Exactly! I'm telling you, it's the daftest thing I've heard since we were kicked out of the Garden of Eden!

Girl   *(Looking up, then glancing left and right to make sure nobody is listening.)* Well, I don't think Noah's ever been terribly bright, dear. I'm told he can only count up to two!

Boy   Well, that may be so, but he's really flipped now! Do you know what he told me?! He told me that it was going to rain for forty days and forty nights and that the whole world would be flooded and that he was building a boat to save his family and us animals!

Girl	Oh, those weather forecasters, they never get it right, do they? Sometimes I think all the money we spend on weather forecasting equipment and on research and development is just totally wasted. Whatever the forecasters say it's going to do, it always does the opposite. I'm beginning to think they just say the first thing that comes into their heads. It'll probably not rain at all, it'll probably be the hottest, driest summer we've . . .
Boy	Will you shut up going on about the weather forecasters! This has nothing to do with the weather forecasters! It wasn't the weather forecasters who said it would rain for forty days and nights, it was Noah!
Girl	Oh, well, maybe it will then.
Boy	Of course it won't! Can you imagine the whole world flooded because of rain? It's absolutely ludicrous! But that's not all he said! He also said that the only people and animals that would survive would be those that went on his boat with him. All the other animals and people would be drowned by the rain!
Girl	Yes, well I suppose that does sound a bit unlikely, dear.
Boy	A bit unlikely?! You can say that again! And do you know what he said then? He said that you and I were to go to his boat tomorrow morning and he would take us with him so that there would always be unicorns! Can you believe it? I'm telling you, that man ought to be in a mental hospital!
Girl	Actually, I don't think they've built any of those, yet, dear.
Boy	Well it's about time they did.
Girl	Anyway, what did you say to him?

Boy	Are you kidding? I humoured him! The man's a nut-case! I'm telling you, those humans are funny enough creatures when they're rational! But when their brains are scrambled you have to be very careful how you handle them!
Girl	So you told him that we would go with him?
Boy	It was the safest thing to do!
Girl	But we're not going to really?
Boy	Are you serious? Of course we're not going with him! In fact, no one is going with him! His stupid great boat is stuck on the top of a mountain, forty miles from the sea! It's not going anywhere! He's not going anywhere! And wherever it is that he's not going, we're certainly not going with him!
Girl	Well, as long as you're sure.
Boy	What do you mean, as long as I'm sure?
Girl	It's just that I'm not a very good swimmer and you know how I hate getting wet.
Boy	Well, we only have two options, either we go to this boat of his tomorrow morning, or we don't. What choice is there to make?
Girl	I'm not sure, call it unicorn's intuition if you like, I just hope we're making the *right* choice.
Boy	You *hope* we're making the right choice! What do you mean, you *hope* we're making the right choice? How could we *possibly* be making the wrong choice? I'm telling you, there'll still be unicorns around long after old Noah's dead and gone!

GROUP DISCUSSION

Life is all about making decisions and having to choose, and often these choices are far from easy. For example, it would seem wonderful if a church were willing to give generously to the needy, but what if that church then had to close through not being able to pay its bills? And would it be good, or not so good, if a man regularly gave generously to the poor to the extent that his own family went hungry? The dilemma arises because of divided loyalties, i.e. we have a responsibility to the needy but we also have a responsibility towards the people who are dependent on us. It must be said, however, that mostly we err on the side of caution!

For this debate the group is being asked to play the part of the Church Council for the Bickrin Methodist Chapel, a difficult task since Bickrin Church Council rarely agrees on anything.

The Chapel's property includes a superb hall which is regularly let out to local groups within the community. Recently, the group which has been using the hall on Friday evenings, the forward-looking 'Bickrin Society of Clairvoyants and Fortune-tellers', has announced that, because of unforeseen circumstances, the society has closed and they will no longer be needing the hall. Word that the hall would, in future, be available on Friday evenings has quickly spread throughout the village and a number of groups have applied for its use. As Church Council members, your job is to discuss the applications received and agree on their order of merit.

1. The Acid Plate-Etching Society (APES) is a small group of enthusiasts who would like to use the hall for their weekly meetings. (Previously, they met in the village hall, but they have had to manage without a meeting place since one of their members knocked over a jar and dissolved a large part of the hall floor.) They have confirmed that they are now fully insured for accidents and they would like to point out that, because the majority of their members are disabled, it is particularly important that the group should continue.

2. The Model Exhibitors And Steam Locomotives Engineering Society (MEASLES) is a recently formed group of railway model engineers which had been meeting in the community centre (until a model of George Stevenson's 'Rocket' tipped over and the community centre was slightly burned down). Despite this early setback, MEASLES seems to be spreading, and they are now looking for a new meeting place. The society has mostly elderly people as its members and they are desperate that this new-found interest and social opportunity should be allowed to continue. They have also confirmed that the running of steam models at the club's meetings is now forbidden in the rules (Rule 23.a.iii).

3. The Young-people's Outward Bound Society (YOBS), was set up some time ago to encourage young people to become involved in Outward Bound activities. Unfortunately, so many young people went missing from the group's expeditions, that it was decided to change YOBS into a more conventional youth club, for which they need the use of the chapel hall. The majority of the children who will attend the youth club are from broken homes (mostly just the windows) so it is important to keep the club going. Unfortunately, funds are short and it must be recognised that the club would not be able to meet the full cost of hiring the hall.

4. The Society for Confabulation And Bible Study (SCABS) is a group from Bickrin Chapel which is newly formed for fellowship and the study of Scripture. Since the group is from the Chapel, it would normally be given preference for the use of the hall and would not, of course, be expected to pay any hire charges. Clearly this would adversely affect the chapel's finances, especially since Friday evenings generate a good rental income. However, previous such groups which have formed from Bickrin Chapel have seldom lasted very long because of the constant niggling disagreements which seem to spring up.